WELCOME
— TO THE —
CLUB BABY BOOK

A JOURNAL FOR YOUR
PARENTING MISADVENTURES

RAQUEL D'APICE

creator of *The Ugly Volvo* blog

CHRONICLE BOOKS
SAN FRANCISCO

ISBN: 978-1-4521-6620-9

Manufactured in China

MIX
Paper from
responsible sources
FSC
www.fsc.org   FSC™ C008047

Design by Lizzie Vaughan and Taylor Roy

10 9 8 7 6 5 4 3 2 1

Chronicle Books LLC
680 Second Street
San Francisco, California 94107
www.chroniclebooks.com

CONTENTS

THIS IS NOT A BABY BOOK.

This is an attempt to capture some of the less-talked-about facets of the child-having experience.

If you decide not to write anything in this book, that is fine. If you decide you would like to answer lots of questions and draw lots of pictures in this book, that is also fine. If you impulsively decide to read through or fill out a few pages while pumping or doing seemingly endless loads of laundry, terrific. Don't stress about it. This book has some traditional baby book pages, but this book is much more about you than it is about your baby.

Having a child is exhausting and keeping a baby book, while a charming idea, is not always a practical one. I would love to write out long, detailed baby books for my children, but most days I am lucky if I remember to eat breakfast and realistically I will be in my mid-70s before I get around to "printing out all those Snapfish pictures."

If you were hoping for a book that asks you to write down specific dates and page after page of developmental information, possibly this is the wrong book for you.

If you were hoping for a book with a page labeled:

TEAR OUT THIS PAGE AND USE IT TO WIPE UP THE SPIT UP ON THE CLEAN SHIRT YOU PUT ON **LITERALLY** TWO MINUTES AGO.

then this is **exactly** the book you are looking for, although we cut that page after my innovative request of "Hey, let's just print the book on paper towels" was turned down.

Being a parent is a wild experience, and while it's nice to have some things written down for posterity, it's more important to savor the moments than to document them. Enjoy parenthood— at least the parts where you are not completely exhausted. Write things down if you want to, but don't put pressure on yourself to do things that make life any crazier than it already is.

OK, so this is, technically, a baby book.

But it's one that understands that your time, like your child, is precious.

1

PREGNANCY
AND THE
EARLY DAYS

WHO KNEW?

Out of everyone you told, who was the most excited to find out you were expecting?

How did you tell them? What was their reaction?

(Ex. My mother's reaction was to smile continuously for the next five months like someone in a 1920s-style lunatic asylum.)

....

....

....

....

....

....

....

....

....

....

BOY OR GIRL?

Did you find out the gender of the baby beforehand? Was it what you were expecting?

....

....

....

....

....

....

....

....

How did you tell people?

☐ GENDER REVEAL PARTY

☐ JUST WALKED UP TO PEOPLE AND WENT
"HEY, WE'RE HAVING A ...."

☐ OTHER ....

....

CRAVINGS

If you were not pregnant, but lived for an extended period alongside a pregnant person, what was the weirdest request they made that you fulfilled?

("Before I get in the car and drive to town at 3AM, you swear to me that you NEED orange soda?")

What was a request to which you had to say no?

("Are you serious, you woke me up in the middle of the night to rub your ears??")

FEELING GREAT!

Here are the parts of being pregnant that were fantastic:

(Ex. Great hair, great skin, general sense of wonder at creating a human life)

1 ....

....

2 ....

....

3 ....

....

....

4 ....

....

....

5 ....

....

....

FEELING . . .

Here are the parts of being pregnant that were, to put it lightly, "less than ideal."

(Ex. Vomiting, swollen feet, sciatica, weight gain, varicose veins, urinating whenever you sneeze, getting sick without being able to take medicine for it, WHY ARE ALL THESE TOTAL STRANGERS TOUCHING MY STOMACH, more sciatica, not being able to shave the bottoms of your legs because you literally can't reach them, sweating, waking up in the middle of the night next to one of those pillows that looks like a giant sandworm and being so uncomfortable you never manage to get back to sleep, back pain, dental problems, constant exhaustion, ok, ok, I should probably let you do a few of these)

1 ....

2 ....

3 ....

4 ....

5 ....

6 ....

7 ....

8 ....

9 ....

10 ....

DON'T TELL ME . . .

What are three things people said to you during your pregnancy that you totally could've done without hearing?

(Insider Tip: The comment "You're so big! Are you having twins?" is particularly unappreciated when the person is not having twins!)

1 ....

....

....

2 ....

....

....

3 ....

....

....

DID SOMEONE SERIOUSLY SAY THAT??????

SHUT UP, FOR REAL???

DID YOU HIT THEM? TELL ME YOU HIT THEM.

☐ I TOTALLY HIT THEM

☐ I WANTED TO HIT THEM BUT I WAS RAISED BETTER THAN THAT

☐ IT NEVER EVEN CROSSED MY MIND TO HIT THEM BECAUSE I'M SURE THEY DIDN'T MEAN ANYTHING BY IT

☐ CAN'T EVEN STOP TO ANSWER THIS QUESTION BECAUSE I AM BUSY STILL HITTING THIS PERSON

BIRTH PLAN

Write down the parts of your well-intentioned birth plan that went right out the window.

(Ex. Had anticipated a drug-free birth in a koi pond set to violin music but wound up getting an epidural/C-section/giving birth in a Toyota)

BIRTH WAS . . .

Ok, so you gave birth and you probably have a lot of feelings about it. If you had to sum up the experience in FIVE WORDS OR PHRASES, what would they be?

(The first ones that come to mind are "surreal," "barely-made-it-to-the-hospital-on-time," and "accidental poop.")

BIRTH DETAILS

I've got this wild feeling like maybe you have one or two more things to say about the whole "birth experience." Some of it may be stuff you're a little anxious about saying out loud (it frequently involves blood and sobbing), but hey, that's why this journal comes with a lock!*

Here's how it went down:

....

....

....

....

....

....

....

....

....

....

....

....

....

*It doesn't, but wouldn't that have been a great idea?

WELCOME TO THE WORLD

What you named the baby:

Other names you considered:

....

....

Name you picked out if baby had been the other gender:

....

....

Names random people kept suggesting that you didn't like but to which you listened politely and nodded and went, "Mmmhmm, those are good ones! I'll definitely keep them in mind!"

....

....

Embarrassing names you liked when you were a teenager:

....

....

WELCOME TO THE WORLD

Why you picked the name you picked:

....

....

Despite how much time you spent agonizing over picking a name, here is the thing you actually call the baby all the time (circle all that apply):

PEANUT   MUNCHKIN   LOVE   CUTIE

SWEET PEA   BABY CAKES   PUMPKIN

BUG   ANGEL   POTATO   GRUMPY PANTS

MUFFIN   SWEETS   BUDDY   MONSTER

And the weird nicknames you've made up

(Ex. Truffle Pig, Grumbledore)

....

....

Explain the origin of at least one of the nicknames

(Due to his habit of moving one of his arms up and down repeatedly like those figurines in Chinese restaurants, I began calling one of my sons "Lucky Cat.")

....

....

....

THOUGHTS TO SHARE WITH YOUR BABY

Dear Baby,

You were born at this time: ....

Here are the people who showed up to welcome you:

....

....

Here's my fantasy lineup of who I wish had been there:

(Ex. Dolly Parton, Fred Rogers, Ellen DeGeneres, Mark Twain)

....

....

Here are relatives I wish had been there to see it (if any):

....

....

Here's the song I wish had been playing right as you came out:

(Ex. Mozart's Marriage of Figaro Overture, Whitney Houston's "I Will Always Love You," that "Y'all ready for this" song from the *Space Jam* soundtrack)

....

Here's some other information about your birth I thought was interesting and/or vaguely important:

....

....

BEST ADVICE

What is the best piece of advice you
got about having a baby?

....

....

....

Who gave it to you? ....

Did you realize at the time that it was great advice?

☐ I DID   ☐ I HAD LITERALLY NO CLUE

If an expectant parent asked you about
having a baby and you could only tell them
three things, what would they be?

1 ....

....

2 ....

....

3 ....

....

UNWANTED ADVICE

Write in a piece of unwanted advice you got from a stranger. Draw in the stranger's face and feel free to make them look totally hideous if it makes you feel better about not taking their annoying advice.

BABY REGISTRY

Above the delivery box, list the things you had to hastily order because you didn't realize you'd need/want them until the baby was already here.

Above the garbage can, list the baby-related things you used to think were super important to have that you now think are totally unnecessary.

(Ex. "So happy about that $200 bassinet that she literally refused to sleep in and which we now use as a makeshift clothes hamper.")

SHOWS YOU BINGE-WATCHED

Having a newborn is completely magical and life changing and also sometimes totally mundane because they do not really do anything.

What shows/podcasts/movies did you binge on to get you through the early months when your child did nothing but sleep, poop, and stare at the ceiling fan?

(Ex. During his paternity leave my husband watched literally every episode of *The X-Files*, including the seasons after David Duchovny and Gillian Anderson had left the show.)

I listened to: I watched:

STRONGER AND TOUGHER

Write about a time when it hit you that both you and the baby
were stronger than you had initially realized.

I learned that I was tougher than I had anticipated when:

....

....

....

....

....

I learned that the baby was tougher than I had anticipated when:

....

....

....

....

....

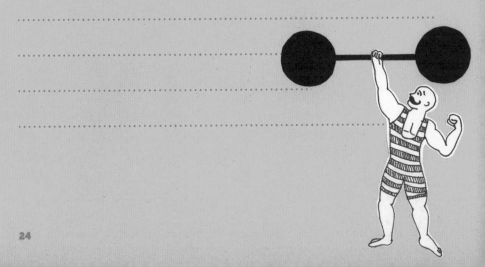

IT HAPPENS TO THE BEST OF US

Check off anything that has happened to you:

- [ ] HELD YOUR CHILD AND PANICKED ABOUT DROPPING THEM

- [ ] PUT YOUR BABY IN SLING/CARRIER AND PANICKED THAT THEY WERE ABOUT TO FALL OUT/SUFFOCATING/GOING TO GET CRUSHED IF YOU YOURSELF TRIPPED AND FELL

- [ ] TRIED TO INSTALL A CAR SEAT AND THE INSTALLATION INSTRUCTIONS WERE ONLY SLIGHTLY LESS CONFUSING THAN LEARNING ORGANIC CHEMISTRY

- [ ] BREASTFED THE BABY AND HAD SOMEONE SAY SOMETHING OBNOXIOUS TO YOU ABOUT IT

- [ ] DECIDED NOT TO BREASTFEED THE BABY AND HAD SOMEONE SAY SOMETHING OBNOXIOUS TO YOU ABOUT IT

- [ ] TURNED YOUR HEAD FOR A MOMENT AND YOUR CHILD ROLLED OFF THE BED/CHANGING TABLE/SOFA

- [ ] MADE A MENTAL NOTE OF SOMETHING THE BABY "DEFINITELY COULDN'T REACH" AND TWO SECONDS LATER IT WAS SOMEHOW IN THEIR HANDS

- [ ] HAD SOMETHING OF YOURS DESTROYED BY THE BABY (THIS CAN BE ANYTHING FROM A CERAMIC VASE TO YOUR SOCIAL LIFE)

SURPRISE!

Here are three facts about parenthood
that you had ZERO IDEA ABOUT
before having children:

1

2

3

ARE YOU TIRED?

At various times during parenthood, various parts of your body will be exhausted. On the figure below, label the parts of your body that hurt right now and explain why.

(Ex. Hair—constantly on the cusp of being ripped out of your neck by your six-month-old who is in a "grabby" phase)

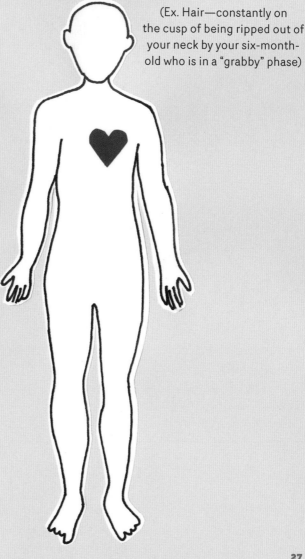

Tell a story that involves one of your child's outfits.

(Ex. An outfit you love. An outfit you hated but it was a gift and you felt obligated to have your child wear it. A time you forgot to pack a backup outfit and your child had an explosive bowel movement and you had to bring them home wrapped in paper towels from a public bathroom.)

SONGS

List any weirdly specific songs you found yourself singing to the baby, even if they are not baby songs.

(Ex. I constantly found myself singing "Walking in Memphis" and Elton John's "I'm Still Standing" to the point where those songs are now inextricably linked with memories of my sons' infancies.)

If you ever made up a song or lullaby that you regularly find yourself singing, write a few of the words here:

Who's someone new that you met through having a kid and it's actually turning out that they are kind of nice and possibly not a complete lunatic?

Include details on either your blossoming relationship or your attempts to "casually run into them."

D'OH!

Describe a time you went out with the baby and FORGOT TO BRING SOMETHING YOU WOUND UP NEEDING.

(Ex. I took my son to a family gathering and went, "We'll be there for 6 hours. Two diapers should definitely be enough!")

....

....

....

....

....

....

....

Did the world end?

☐ YES

☐ NO

☐ OK, OK, NO, BUT IT SEEMED LIKE IT DID AT THE TIME

TO THE DOCTOR

Describe any random pediatrician's visit. Did they get shots? Was the office full of screaming babies? Did the waiting room have *Highlights* magazine or that wooden bead rollercoaster/ maze toy that's in every pediatrician's office?

The thing about this visit I most want to remember is:

....

....

....

The part I'd most like to forget is:

....

....

....

BOWEL MOVEMENTS

Check off any of the below that have happened to you:

☐ CHILD HAS BOWEL MOVEMENT THAT REQUIRES DISPOSING OF, RATHER THAN WASHING, AN OUTFIT

☐ CHILD HAS BOWEL MOVEMENT THAT GOES ALL THE WAY UP THEIR BACK (TWO CHECK MARKS IF IT REACHED THEIR HAIR)

☐ CHILD HAS BOWEL MOVEMENT THAT GOES ALL THE WAY DOWN AND FILLS THEIR SOCKS

☐ CHILD IS CONSTIPATED AND PASSES SOMETHING THAT IS THE SIZE AND CONSISTENCY OF A SOFTBALL

☐ CHILD POOPS IN BATHTUB

☐ CHILD POOPS ON FLOOR

☐ CHILD SPRAYS POOP EVERYWHERE LIKE A BOMBARDIER BEETLE

☐ CHILD SPITS UP MILK ONTO THEMSELVES TWO SECONDS AFTER YOU HAVE CHANGED THEIR OUTFIT

☐ CHILD SPITS UP MILK ONTO YOU TWO SECONDS AFTER YOU HAVE SHOWERED AND GOTTEN DRESSED

☐ CHILD SPITS UP MILK AND/OR SNEEZES INTO YOUR MOUTH

CANCELLED PLANS

Did you recently cancel some plans that you had been looking forward to because of the baby? This is obviously a rhetorical question. What were the plans?

....

....

....

....

....

....

....

....

....

....

....

....

....

....

FAKE CANCELLED PLANS

Did you recently weasel your way out of something
you hadn't wanted to go to because of the baby? What
was it and what was the excuse you made up? How
guilty did you feel? How totally relieved and fantastic
did you feel right after cancelling? I know, right?

I AM SO SORRY BUT . . .

CRAZY RELATIVES

Do you have a relative who's been driving you COMPLETELY UP THE WALL since the baby was born?

Write about them here but call them Old Uncle Sophocles and write everything in code in case they find this book.

WHO YOU GONNA CALL?

Who has been surprisingly helpful?

(Ex. I have an aunt who has helped out with childcare so often I am fairly sure I owe her either an all-expenses-paid trip to Barbados or possibly a kidney.)

If you could fully thank them in three sentences, what would you say?

Who are the people you call when you're super stressed and at the end of your rope?

List their names (and if you need to, their phone numbers) here because having a child is nothing if not an exercise in constantly feeling like you're at the end of your rope and it's good to have this list close at hand to remember to reach out.

2

EVERYTHING

OK SO FAR?

Before you had kids, what did you think having a child would be like?

(Ex. I now know that it is heart-wrenching and indescribable but going in I figured it would be sort of like getting a kitten.)

....

....

....

....

....

....

....

....

....

....

Draw how freaking lonely being at home
with a newborn can sometimes feel.

Even though you second-guess everything you do and your energy level is that of an almost completely drained smartphone battery, you are seriously doing a wonderful job as a parent.

What is an award you'd like to give yourself?

(Ex. The "I took care of a baby while simultaneously having food poisoning" award, or the "I somehow made it through Tuesday without hurling a box of crackers at the wall in anger" award)

Without telling them anything about this page, have a friend give you the words to fill in the blanks and then read the letter aloud.

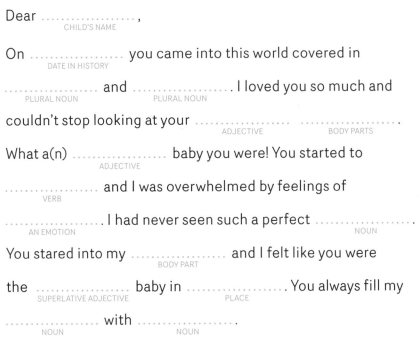

Dear . . . . ,
      CHILD'S NAME

On . . . . you came into this world covered in
  DATE IN HISTORY

. . . . and . . . . I loved you so much and
   PLURAL NOUN   PLURAL NOUN

couldn't stop looking at your . . . .
                      ADJECTIVE   BODY PARTS

What a(n) . . . . baby you were! You started to
         ADJECTIVE

. . . . and I was overwhelmed by feelings of
   VERB

. . . . I had never seen such a perfect . . . .
  AN EMOTION   NOUN

You stared into my . . . . and I felt like you were
                   BODY PART

the . . . . baby in . . . . You always fill my
   SUPERLATIVE ADJECTIVE   PLACE

. . . . with . . . .
   NOUN   NOUN

Much love,

. . . .
  A NAME

(Fun fact: I tried this out to see what I'd get and ended up with the final line "You always fill my teacup with sperm.")

What are three ways in which you think about things differently now that you have a child?

(Ex. I'm more tolerant of other people's children screaming in parks and more conscientious about the world I'm leaving for my children (and my children's children) and also I can immediately tell when a three-year-old is about to poop herself.)

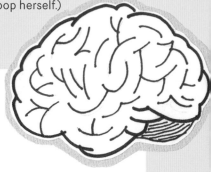

Name five things, which, if you could go back to
being childless for a day, you promise yourself
you would never again take for granted.

(Ex. Two of my top ones are "drinking coffee while it is still hot" [I vaguely
remember this being something I once did??] and "living places without caring
whether the schools are good in that area.")

1 ....

....

2 ....

....

3 ....

....

4 ....

....

5 ....

....

ENJOYABLE COFFEE   TEPID BROWN SLUDGE

Write a few haiku poems about taking care of a baby.

(A haiku is a non-rhyming three-line poem, first line being five syllables,
second line being seven syllables, and the last being five syllables again.)

Example:

Why are my house keys
Inside the recycling bin?
Get over here now.

DEAR CO-PARENT

Parenting with someone else is hard because you love the other person so,
so much but also you sometimes feel like you are going to have a complete
mental breakdown and throw all their belongings out of a car.

Below, write out the things they do that are bothering you.

DEAR CO-PARENT,

I LOVE YOU BUT HERE ARE SOME THINGS I NEED YOU TO STOP, OR IN SOME

CASES START, DOING: ....

....

....

....

....

....

....

....

....

....

On this page write out the things they do for you or your child that make you love and appreciate them.

Big things. Small gestures. Make the list as specific as possible. If they're willing, have them write out the same lists for you.

DEAR CO-PARENT,

HERE IS WHY YOU ARE AN AMAZING HUMAN BEING:

If you are raising kids as a single parent (or get
so little help you often feel like a single parent)
what's something you wish you could make
people in two-parent families understand?

....

....

....

....

....

What's a challenge about single parenthood that you had no idea about going in?

(Ex. The challenge of being a single mother trying to explain to a young son
how to urinate standing up using body parts that you yourself do not have.)

....

....

....

....

....

....

When was the first time you spent a night away from the baby?

....

....

....

How did it go?

....

....

What did you do?

....

....

Was it harder on you or the baby?

(Acceptable answers include "I have a five-year-old and have still not managed to spend a night away because I am terrified" and "I left my nine-month-old with relatives for a week and part of me wished I could leave her there for a full month.")

....

....

....

When you were a kid did you know you wanted kids?

How many did you think you wanted?

Now that you're an adult how many
do you think you want?

Are you saying this before or after having given birth at least once?

If you're currently caring for a baby, how many
times a day do you think, "Maybe I should've
just gotten a beautiful golden retriever and
moved to Seattle and become a novelist?"

If you currently live in Seattle and/or are a novelist, where's the fantasy place
you'd move to with your no kids and beautiful golden retriever?

Step 1:

Place a crayon in your fist.

Step 2:

Pressing down HARD, scribble all over this page with an intensity that denotes how frustrated you sometimes feel because raising kids is occasionally maddening.

Step 3

Sign and date the drawing. If you are so inclined, hang it on your fridge.

On this diagram of the ocean, use an arrow to mark how totally underwater you feel all the time.

Where the snorklers are

Lots of fish and sharks and stuff

Honestly not sure what happens here

Giant squid and those creepy fish with the lights in their heads

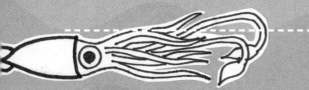

Titanic

Mariana trench (deepest part of the ocean)

Things are different after you have a baby, and a lot of things you remember from your previous life are gone.

On the tombstones, write the things you miss from your pre-baby existence.

(Ex. R.I.P. Having Disposable Income)

R.I.P

R.I.P

R.I.P

R.I.P

BACK TO WORK! :)

You are going back to work outside the home.
Make a list of why this is amazing and wonderful.

It is fantastic because:

BACK TO WORK! :(

You are going back to work outside the home.
Make a list of why this is completely heartbreaking.

It is emotionally crippling and I feel as though I may never recover because:

....

....

....

....

....

....

....

....

....

....

....

....

....

Color in this cry for help.

PARENTING HAS

I AM IN DESPERAT

THANK

When you need help because parenting is exhausting and you are overwhelmed, go find someone who can help you and patiently hold this sign in front of their face until they get the hint. If needed, tear this sign out and permanently tape it to the refrigerator.

BECOME OVERWHELMING AND
NEED OF ASSISTANCE.
OU

DAYDREAMING

Fantasy situation page! For some reason you find yourself childless for ONE MONTH but know that your child is happy and taken care of. What do you do? Besides sleep past 6AM. Obviously you do that. But what else?

In the talking balloons, write in the things you WISH someone would say to you that no one has been saying.

(Ex. "Please, let ME unload the dishwasher! You are doing more than enough already!")

What is something for which you are incredibly grateful?

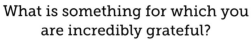

PRE-BABY LOVES

What are three things you loved doing before children that are sort of ruined now?

(Ex. "Traveling" or "Having a white couch")

What are three seemingly small things your child does that make you fall head-over-heels in love with them every time?

(Ex. When he hugs other children, when he asks to wear a tie "like his grandpa," when he pretends to be two characters having a conversation and gives one of them a high-up falsetto voice to differentiate it from the other one.)

A BETTER PERSON

What are three ways in which having children has made you a better person?

(Acceptable answers can be anything from "I am constantly overwhelmed by a love I did not realize I was capable of feeling" to "I can calmly make an omelet while someone is vomiting on my neck.")

3

THE
COMPLEXITIES
OF
BABYHOOD

TANTRUMS

Describe a god-awful tantrum/emotional breakdown your child had. Where were you? How did you feel? Any ideas what caused it?

(The answer "Nothing caused it and it remains unexplained to this day" is totally acceptable here.)

REGRETS, I'VE HAD A FEW

What's something that happened with your baby/child over which you're still beating yourself up because you wish you'd handled it differently?

(Ex. Anything from "I wish I had continued breastfeeding" to "I shouldn't have put her in daycare" to "Well maybe we wouldn't be at the pediatrician asking them to pull this raisin out of his nose if I HAD BEEN PAYING ATTENTION.")

....

....

....

....

....

....

....

....

....

....

....

....

BE NICE TO YOURSELF

That??? That is nothing!! Please don't beat yourself up over THAT. You are trying so hard and your child is—listen to me when I say this—lucky to have you as a parent. Are you listening? *pulls you close until we are standing nose to nose*

YOU ARE DOING A FANTASTIC JOB AT SOMETHING THAT IS REALLY, REALLY DIFFICULT. DO NOT BE SO HARD ON YOURSELF.

EDUCATIONAL TOYS

Your child is the lucky recipient of who-even-knows-how-many amazing, wonderful, and sometimes educational toys.

What do they play with instead?

☐ THE TELEVISION REMOTE CONTROL

☐ EVERY CARDBOARD BOX

☐ MY KEYS

☐ ANYTHING THEY FIND IN THE RECYCLING BIN

☐ THE TOILET PAPER AND/OR THE CARDBOARD TOILET PAPER ROLL

☐ MY CHILD OBSESSIVELY COLLECTS ROCKS AND STICKS

☐ ALL THIS OTHER RANDOM NONSENSE:

....

....

....

....

Draw what your child wants to play with more than anything else in the house.

WHAT'S IN YOUR MOUTH?

Draw the worst thing you've ever pulled out of your child's mouth. If you're terrible at drawing, write what it is beneath the sketch.

TOY STORIES

What's something someone else gave them
that you hid/gave away/lost on purpose?

. . . .

What's something that literally everyone keeps
buying for you and now you have like 50 of them?

(Ex. We've gotten so many "lovies" [blankets with animal heads] from people
that I often fantasize about throwing them into a bonfire.)

. . . .

What was something you got your child where you
thought, "Oh boy, I cannot wait to give them this!"
and they looked at it once and were like "Eh."

. . . .

What's a toy you wanted as a kid that
you now realize was total garbage?

. . . .

What's something you really want
your child to like/play with?

. . . .

GIFTS

You probably received a bunch of gifts that were wonderful and super helpful and then a lot of gifts you didn't need and didn't ask for and which (despite the giver's good intentions) you didn't particularly want. Having to write thank you notes for these gifts is sometimes frustrating.

Think of the worst gift you got and below, write the note you really wanted to write.

DEAR .... ,

....

....

....

....

....

....

....

PARENTING LIST

Check off how frequently these have happened to you.

Some total stranger gives you aggressive, unsolicited advice about how to take care of your baby

☐ NEVER　　☐ OK, ONE TIME　　☐ AT LEAST ONCE A WEEK　　☐ EVERY. FREAKING. DAY.

You go on a date and talk about your kid the whole time

☐ EVERY TIME　　☐ OH NO, NEVER

You attempt to have a focused, interesting conversation with another adult while you are also watching a baby and fail miserably

☐ EVERY TIME　　☐ OH NO, NEVER

You shyly approach or want to approach another parent because they seem cool and you'd like to be friends with them

☐ NEVER　　☐ OK, ONE TIME　　☐ AT LEAST ONCE A WEEK　　☐ EVERY. FREAKING. DAY.

You get super excited about some meetup/playdate that winds up being cancelled at the last minute

☐ NEVER　　☐ OK, ONE TIME　　☐ AT LEAST ONCE A WEEK　　☐ EVERY. FREAKING. DAY.

You post a photo of your child to social media and it gets more likes than anything you've ever done

☐ NEVER　　☐ OK, ONE TIME　　☐ AT LEAST ONCE A WEEK　　☐ EVERY. FREAKING. DAY.

The baby sleeps a little longer than they normally sleep and you get so nervous that something's wrong that you go over to check things out and inevitably wake them up with your presence

☐ NEVER　　☐ OK, ONE TIME　　☐ AT LEAST ONCE A WEEK　　☐ EVERY. FREAKING. DAY.

Before having a kid, what were some of the things you were SUPER looking forward to doing with your kid?

(Ex. I'm 90 percent sure I had a child because I wanted to introduce someone to the Little House on the Prairie books and/or the Indiana Jones trilogy.)

I was super excited to:

1 ....

....

2 ....

....

3 ....

....

Have you taken your child to a restaurant?

☐ I DID

☐ NO, I'M TOO TERRIFIED OF WHAT'LL HAPPEN

How did it go?

☐ IT WENT FINE

☐ I CAN NEVER SHOW MY FACE THERE AGAIN

Details from the visit:

....

....

....

....

....

....

Have you taken your child on an airplane?

☐ I DID

☐ THERE ISN'T ENOUGH ANXIETY MEDICATION IN THE WORLD TO GET ME TO DO THIS

How did it go?

☐ WASN'T AS BAD AS I THOUGHT

☐ NEXT TIME I CONSIDER DOING THAT REMIND ME TO OPT FOR SOMETHING LESS PAINFUL, LIKE A ROOT CANAL PERFORMED BY AN UNTRAINED GAS STATION ATTENDANT

Details, assuming you haven't blocked them out:

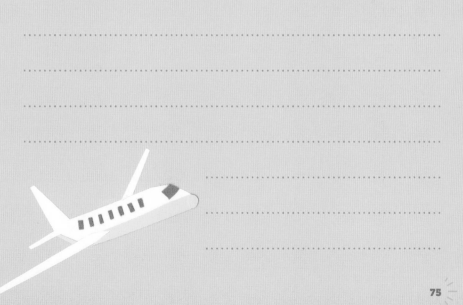

BREASTFEEDING

If you breastfed, in the chart below list the things you totally loved about breastfeeding, and the parts where you were like, "Ugh, I forgot how parts of this can be kind of terrible."

(Ex. The intense closeness you feel when you nurse your baby vs. the inherent [sort of creepy] weirdness when an older child wants to switch breasts and literally says the words, "Other side.")

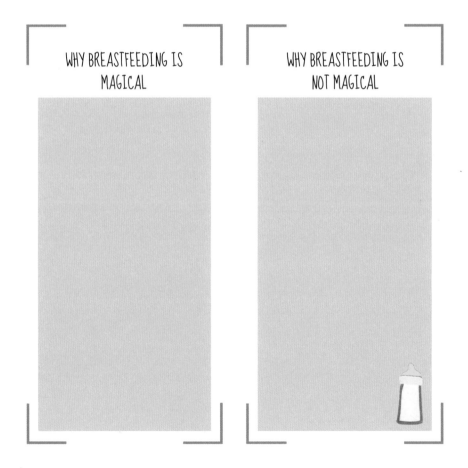

WHY BREASTFEEDING IS MAGICAL

WHY BREASTFEEDING IS NOT MAGICAL

I WILL NEVER DO THAT!

List three things your parents always did when you were a kid where you went, "Ugh, I am never doing those things if I become a parent!" and now that you have kids you do them constantly.

(Ex. I not only accidentally call my sons by each other's names, I also occasionally call them by the dog's name.)

NEW FRIENDS!

Congratulations, your child has made little, tiny, adorable friends!

List a few of their names or write a little bit about them here. What is each one like now and what do you think they'll be like when they grow up?

Child 1:

Child 2:

Child 3:

Are there any parents that you like hanging out with so you have your kids play together even though it's becoming fairly clear that the kids don't particularly care for one another? Or the reverse situation? Cool, me too!

NEWS OF THE DAY

What's a big news story that happened while your child was a baby? Was it something that affected you at all?

EXTRA EXTRA
HERE'S WHAT HAPPENED

PARENTING CHECKLIST

Check the box if this is something you've done:

☐ ACCIDENTALLY CUT YOUR CHILD WHILE CLIPPING THEIR NAILS

☐ FREAKED OUT A LITTLE BECAUSE SOME OTHER KID YOUR CHILD'S AGE WAS DOING SOMETHING YOUR CHILD HADN'T MASTERED YET

☐ LOST YOUR CHILD IN A SUPERMARKET/PLAYGROUND/ETC AND IT LITERALLY FELT LIKE YOUR HEART STOPPED BEATING UNTIL YOU FOUND THEM AGAIN

☐ TOOK CARE OF YOUR CHILD WHILE YOU YOURSELF WERE SICK OR INJURED

☐ WERE SO FRUSTRATED/OVERWHELMED BY EVERYTHING YOU WANTED TO SCREAM AND/OR YOU DID SCREAM

☐ DROVE SOMEWHERE WHILE YOUR CHILD SCREAMED THE WHOLE TIME

☐ BRIBED YOUR CHILD

☐ STARTED GOING TO SLEEP AT 8PM BECAUSE IT'S THE ONLY WAY YOU CAN FUNCTION WITH ANY SORT OF EFFICACY

TOO ADORABLE

Write about something your child was doing that was so adorable you ran out of the room to get something so you could film it and literally the second you hit "record" they stopped whatever they had been doing and stared at you blankly for three minutes.

WHO DO THEY LOOK LIKE?

Write down who the child looks like at:

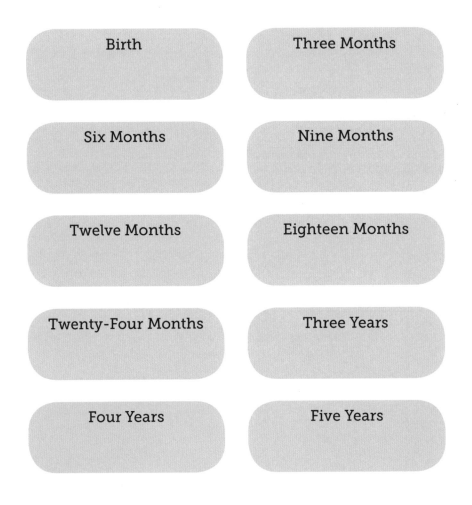

Birth

Three Months

Six Months

Nine Months

Twelve Months

Eighteen Months

Twenty-Four Months

Three Years

Four Years

Five Years

Fun tip! The answer at no point has to be either of the child's parents.

POOP STORIES

You have a poop story that is beyond disgusting. Tell it here.

(Ex. The time I cut the onesie off his body with scissors and threw it in the garbage.)

MORE POOP STORIES

Remember how bad that other poop story seemed? And then THIS one happened.

(You can also substitute horrific stories including other bodily fluids, such as "the time my son urinated into his own eyes," or "the time my son urinated into the dog's eyes," or "the time my son urinated into the dog's mouth," all of which are real things that have actually happened.)

THREE POSITIVE TRAITS

Pick three traits you hope your child has as an adult.

1 ....

....

2 ....

....

3 ....

....

What's a trait you have that you don't want your child to wind up with under any circumstances?

What's something that happened recently that made having a child feel completely impossible and overwhelming?

Date the page ....

THE SWEETEST THING

Write about something that happened
this week with your child that almost
made you tear up it was so sweet.

....

....

....

....

....

....

....

....

....

....

....

....

Date the page ....

FIRST WORD

Write your child's first word inside the wreath.

How did you envision sleep training would go?

How did it actually go?

(If you don't feel like writing it out you can just scribble on this page angrily.)

MORE SLEEP

Here's an expert telling you that if you would only read his book, your baby would effortlessly sleep through the night like all the babies do in Denmark/Sweden/France/Some Other Country Where Everything is Allegedly Perfect.

Draw all the arrows you would like to shoot into his body.

RIDICULOUS THINGS I'VE GOOGLE SEARCHED

Having a child in today's world inevitably requires typing endless child-related questions into search engines. The next time you frantically open your web browser to type in "IS BABY EATS HIS OWN BAND-AID DANGEROUS" write it in here as well, so in 12 years you can laugh about it.

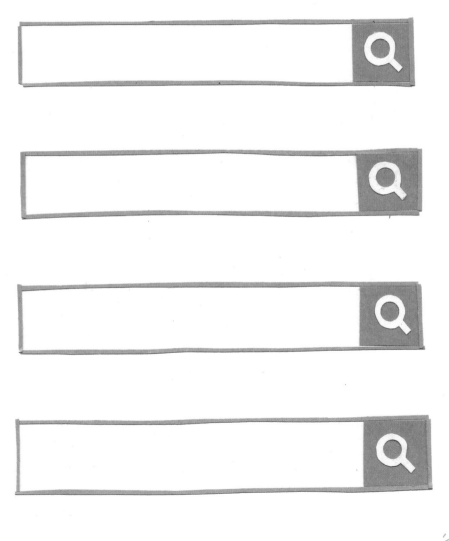

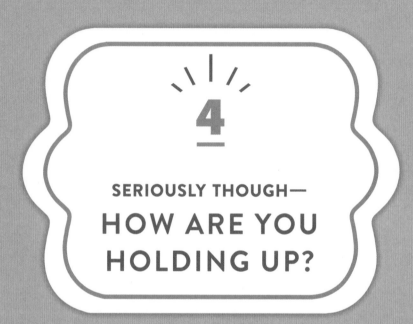

4

SERIOUSLY THOUGH—

HOW ARE YOU HOLDING UP?

I HEREBY SENTENCE YOU TO . . .

Parenting is both a wonderful bonding experience and an endless,
Sisyphean cycle of housework.

Is there a thankless task you feel like you do every
day? (*cough* laundry *cough*) Write one in and
then make a prison tally mark on this page every time
you have to do it. See how quickly the page gets filled.

The boring task I can't stand is:

....

ANOTHER DAY OLDER

Tape in one of your gray hairs. On the opposite page, tell a story about something that happened with your child that may have been the cause of it.

ANOTHER DAY OLDER

....

....

....

....

....

....

....

....

....

....

....

....

....

....

....

....

....

TRAVEL

Here is a map of the world. List the top three places
you want to visit (sans children) on the lines provided
and (using a red pen if you have one) draw hearts on
any other places you're hoping to get to eventually.

Revisit this page in your late 60s/early 70s.

1 ....

2 ....

3 ....

INSPIRE ME

In the space below, write in whatever inspirational
quote gets you through the day (regardless
of whether it's even about parenting).

This week mine has been: "If you've told a child a thousand times and
he still does not understand, then it is not the child who is the slow learner."
–Walter Barbee

In the center of the maze, write in a place you dread being stuck with a child (Ex. the American Girl doll store) and then do your best to get out of there with any remnants of your sanity.

HELP, GET ME OUT OF THIS

. . . .

(insert place you hate bringing your child)

THE PERFECT LIFE

Below, paste in or describe a magazine photo you looked at longingly because everything in it looked perfect.

(A beautifully decorated room, a flawless outfit on a perfectly-in-shape person, a super photogenic children's birthday party)

Using black pen or marker, deface it to remind yourself not to compare yourself to a ridiculous standard that isn't real.

In the white spaces, write in the names of annoying characters from shows your child watches (and/or books and movies) at whom you would like to throw darts. Fill in as many as you can now and add others as you think of them.

THREE WISHES

A genie shows up and offers to make three
aspects of parenting easier. What do you pick?

1 ....

....

2 ....

....

3 ....

....

WHAT CHANGED IN MY LIFE

What are three ways in which your life changed (or is going to change) after having kids that you're still coming to terms with?

Draw your heart as it was for most of your life.
Be as creative or uncreative as you want.

(Ex. Average-size and frequently broken)

Draw your heart now that you have a kid.

(Mine is big but super complicated and always a little bit in pain.)

BREAKDOWN

Color in this woman having a total emotional breakdown outside a supermarket.

The next time you feel like screaming, come here and write out the scream.

Make it as long as you need. Don't hold back.

WHAT I WISH I HAD DONE TODAY

Anyone caring for a baby full time hates the question "What did you do today?" because the day was endless and exhausting and hard and yet when asked to recount your actions you cannot think of a single thing worth mentioning.

If you don't feel like listing the mundane things you did with the baby, make up a list of the things you wish you had done.

(Ex. I learned about medicinal plants, redirected an asteroid that was hurtling toward earth, read a biography of Robert Moses, enrolled in an archery tournament, learned French, taught a gorilla to interact with humans using sign language, took a pottery class, and went back to school to get my MBA.) Read the list whenever people ask about your day.

1 ....

2 ....

3 ....

4 ....

5 ....

6 ....

7 ....

GUILT

Here are things about which you feel HORRIFICALLY GUILTY:

1 ....

2 ....

3 ....

4 ....

5 ....

6 ....

7 ....

8 ....

9 ....

10 ....

11 ....

12 ....

13 ....

14 ....

15 ....

GUILT

16 ....

17 ....

18 ....

19 ....

20 ....

21 ....

22 ....

23 ....

24 ....

25 ....

26 ....

27 ....

28 ....

29 ....

I am KIDDING. I seriously, seriously hope you don't feel guilty about that many things. Please use these pages to write short notes to your child about how much you love them. Or draw pictures of squirrels. Or trace your hands. Or, if you actually feel guilty about that much stuff, you can use these pages to log visits to your therapist.

I FEEL LIKE A SUPERHERO

What about parenting makes you feel like a total superhero?

(Ex. When I manage to get kids to laugh and forget that they were upset about something I want to stand on a hilltop and shout, "Behold, my ability to make a toddler realize that a broken pretzel does not justify thirty minutes of sobbing/hysterically kicking a door!")

BUT MOSTLY I'M NOT

What about parenthood makes you feel totally pathetic and inadequate?

(Ex. Literally everything except the one thing
I listed for the superhero question)

UGH, WHY IS IT SO HARD ???

. . .

UGH

It is so hard because

....

And because

....

And because

....

And because

....

long, exhausted sigh

PERFECT DAY

Describe your perfect day spent with your child.

(Ex. Pancakes, ferry rides, and going to
a museum where nobody has a meltdown)

Describe your perfect day spent without them.

(Ex. I wake up in a beautiful, rural New Zealand town and spend
the day intermittently writing a novel and taking naps.)

....

....

....

....

....

....

....

....

....

....

....

5

THE
ART
OF HAVING A
CHILD

A SHOULDER TO CRY ON

Children can be maddening and some days you need a shoulder to cry on.

Depending on whose shoulder you'd like it to be, cut a face out of a magazine or an old photo album and paste it in the spot provided. Below, tell this person about something that was sort of rough this week.

What books do you read to your child?

Name three you love reading together.

Name three books your child loves that are so long and/or boring that reading them makes you want to cry and beat yourself over the head with a Sophie la girafe.

YES,
THIS ONE
AGAIN

FAVORITE FOODS

What types of foods had you hoped your child would eat? What types of foods do they actually eat?

(Ex. I had hoped my children would eat anything other than just bread and cheese-flavored crackers and whenever that happens it's fantastic.)

WHO ARE YOU LIKE?

How is your child like you when you were little? How are they different?

(Ex. I was painfully shy as a child, whereas my son will happily walk up to complete strangers in Manhattan and say, "HELLO, DO YOU HAVE ANY LOLLIPOPS I COULD HAVE?")

Traits:

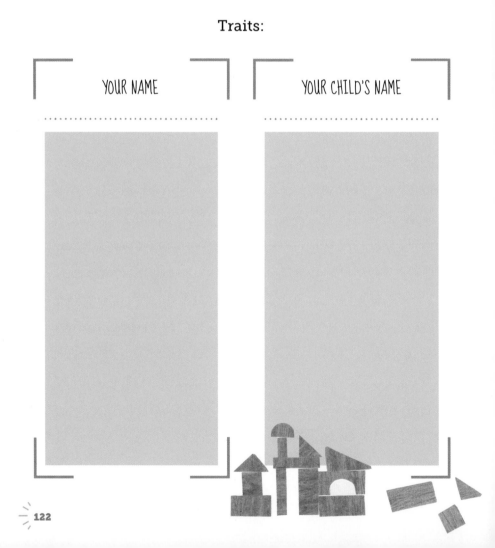

YOUR NAME

YOUR CHILD'S NAME

What are some things that scare your child?
What do you say/do to try and comfort them?

What are some things that scare you about
parenting? How do you try and comfort yourself?

HOW MUCH
COLLEGE
WILL COST

What's something you didn't totally love but you let your child get away with because you were too tired to get into a fight over it?

(Ex. My son really wanted to lick the condensation off the living room windows and part of me was like "Ugh, that's gross," and the other part was like, "I'm sorry, I'm too exhausted to care.")

PERSONALITY

What are some traits you've noticed in your child?

Circle all that apply. Circle your favorite one a bunch of times.

PERSISTENT, HESITANT, CHEERFUL, THOUGHTFUL, CURIOUS,

SHY, OUTGOING, FEARLESS, CAUTIOUS, SERIOUS, ANGRY,

BOISTEROUS, LOVING, FICKLE, REFLECTIVE, ATHLETIC,

GOOFY, LOQUACIOUS, LOGICAL, INSANE, ARTISTIC, DARING,

WORRIED, CONFUSED, LOUD, WEIRD, ENERGETIC, QUIET,

COORDINATED, CREATIVE, ENTHUSIASTIC, JOYFUL, WILD

Write in more detail about the trait you love the most.

....

....

Write about the trait that causes you the most stress.

....

....

OBSESSED WITH MOVIES

Write down the movies or shows that your child is completely obsessed with at:

18 MONTHS ....

24 MONTHS ....

3 YEARS ....

4 YEARS ....

5 YEARS ....

(Ex. When my son was 18 months the only animated movie we owned was *Tarzan* so needless to say we have seen *Tarzan* one hundred million times.)

What's a movie that you and your child love watching together?

....

What's a movie that your child loves that it kills you to watch because the movie is so bad?

....

A LOT OF CUTE

What words does your child pronounce
incorrectly that you sometimes don't correct
because the mispronunciations are so cute?

I'M SO GROSS

What are three of the grossest things you've done since having a child that you never in a million years would've done before parenthood?

(Ex. I once caught my child's vomit in my cupped hands to save a friend's couch.)

1 ....

....

....

2 ....

....

....

3 ....

....

....

What are questions your child has asked or statements they've made that you couldn't stop telling people about because they were adorable/weird/humiliating/hilarious?

Come back to this page whenever they come up with a new one and write them out here.

Example:

Kid: Is that the doctor?

My Mother: That's the doctor's assistant.

Kid: What's an assistant?

My Mother: An assistant is someone who helps out another person.

Kid: (turning to me) You are my assistant?

Me: Basically, yes.

Why might you want another child?

(Acceptable answers vary greatly and include everything from "to give my first child a sibling" to things like "you could not pay me enough money to have another child" and "help with farm work.")

What are a few reasons why you don't want another child?

(Note: I myself had many in-depth answers to this question and still wound up having a second child.)

DRESS UP!

What character(s) does your child constantly pretend to be (a pirate, Elsa, Spiderman, etc.)?

My son regularly insists that he's "a Jedi" or "a really sweet baby rattlesnake named Derek," so please don't leave out the weird ones.)

1 ....

2 ....

3 ....

4 ....

IT'S A GREAT COSTUME, BUT IT'S NOT APPROPRIATE FOR YOUR AUNT'S WEDDING.

FAMILY TRADITIONS

What are a few family traditions you've started or wanted to start?

(Ex. We sit on the sofa and watch BBC Nature documentaries together on the weekends to the point where David Attenborough's voice narrates my dreams.)

SOME ADVICE

What advice do you want to give your child
for the future? Pick the three pieces of advice
you think are the most important.

1 ....

....

2 ....

....

3 ....

....

THE PERFECT SHOT

Tape in a photo that turned out
exactly as you hoped it would.

NOT PERFECT, BUT THE BEST

Tape in a photo where nothing went the way you hoped it was going to go.

Look at it for a while before realizing that, in its own way, it is also a fantastic photo.

WORTHWHILE

As completely insane as life with children feels
most of the time, what was one of the moments
that made you feel like it was all worth it?

....

....

....

....

....

....

....

....

....

....

....

....

....

....

....

A LETTER TO MY CHILD

Write a letter to your child.

ONE LAST WORD OF ADVICE

If your child someday finds this book and you want to be sure they come away with ONE thing, what would it be?